£ 2.99
N 40
TK

Anna Saunders

Ghosting for Beginners

Indigo Dreams Publishing

First Edition: Ghosting for Beginners
First published in Great Britain in 2018 by:
Indigo Dreams Publishing
24, Forest Houses
Cookworthy Moor
Halwill
Beaworthy
Devon
EX21 5UU

www.indigodreams.co.uk

Anna Saunders has asserted her right under the Copyright, Designs and Patents Act 1988 to be identified as the author of this work.
© 2018 Anna Saunders

ISBN 978-1-910834-81-7

British Library Cataloguing in Publication Data. A CIP record for this book can be obtained from the British Library.

Designed and typeset in Palatino Linotype by Indigo Dreams.

Cover design by Ronnie Goodyer.
Printed and bound in Great Britain by 4edge Ltd.

Papers used by Indigo Dreams are recyclable products made from wood grown in sustainable forests following the guidance of the Forest Stewardship Council.

to Sheila Saunders

Acknowledgements

My thanks go to the following publications for publishing some of these poems: Amarillis, Eyeflash Magazine, New Walk Magazine, ENVOI, Fenland Reed Magazine, Atrium, Proletariat Poetry, Prole, Riggwelter, Ink Sweat and Tears, An Algebra of Owls, Critical Quarterly, Hedgehog Press; and to the Battered Moon Poetry Competition 2017 for awarding me Second Prize for A Trick of the Eye, and to the Festival of Firsts Competition 2017 for awarding me First Prize for Orpheus Ruins the Party.

Thank you to all my supportive poetry friends, to those of you who have been the inspiration for some of these poems and to Christine Whittemore and my wonderful mother, Sheila Saunders, for constructive and encouraging editorial guidance.

Thank you to the ever inspiring and generous-hearted Ronnie and Dawn, of Indigo Dreams for publishing this and my previous collection Burne Jones and the Fox.

Also by Anna Saunders:

Burne Jones and the Fox, IDP, 2016
Kissing the She Bear, Wild Conversations Press, 2015
Struck, Pindrop Press, 2014
Communion, Wild Conversations Press, 2010

CONTENTS

Ghosting for Beginners

Orpheus Ruins the Party
(The trial of Orpheus' killers)

In their defence the accused say he quashed
the mood of bonhomie,
extinguished their fire with a dirge
trickled slow and cold from his lyre.

The Defence say,
let's hear more about the deceased,
a man who walked the lanes lamenting,
singing always the same, tired song.

No one invited him for this, to spill dark music
so it pooled like a shadow.
Even the birds became nervy,
skittering as they heard his step.

Where is that man who made the damsels
open like flowers at dawn,
the men gambol and carouse?

The mouth of the wind is stopped
as they fall upon him.

In summing up the Defence say how incendiary
the display of sorrow is,
that grief is a fire that must be snuffed out
before it spreads.

The judge shrugs,
recalls how only yesterday
that he'd kicked a cup from a beggar.

Coins roll on stone.
Orpheus' limbs bob on the river's floor.

The killers walk free, heads held high.
They remember, only after he is buried,

how thirsty the soil was once for his song,
how the cracked earth drank it greedily,
as if it were rain after a time of drought.

Wood Garlic

In the darkness of the ancient woods
a galaxy of fragile constellations –
the spiked flowers of the *ramsoms*.

The bulbs once harvested for Hecate,
brushed smooth of soil,
placed on rocks for the moon goddess.

Bear Leaf – its other name.

Can you imagine the furred beast – talons
like scissors, ripping the stitch of root
from the dark weave of earth?

What a plant! Those delicate blooms,
mimicking the heavens
coupled with that smell –
salty, ripe, heady as hot flesh.
The body's incense, smouldering.

Aren't we all wild garlic
rooted into the dark woods

offering ourselves to the gods,
cowering from rough paws,
blazing our pure stars?

The Lapwing

*Myth has it that a maid was turned into a lapwing by her mistress as
a punishment for stealing a pair of scissors.*

Is it the wing-music that makes you lift your gaze?
The throb of the flight feathers as it soars?

You caught her stealing, your punishment
was to cast her to the sky.

It was black and white at first, wasn't it? Closer,
you see the colour merge and meld; bottle green, mottled,
marbled with bronze.

You took the earth,
made of her a winged exile,
thought you committed no crime.

Too late for remorse now
as the blades of her wings cut the cloth of the sky
and her eerie call haunts you.

We cannot escape our sins,
they hang, feathered, above us,

and even when we sit alone, in silence,
their plaintive song echoes in our ears.

To the Naturalist on Valentine's Day

The rose stands in the thin vase,
its stem is like a amputated tail
cocooned
in a fluid reserve.

Go and apologise to the trees
for what we have done.
Lopped them down for lumber
crushed their pulp for cards.

When you reach into the split bark
there is a faint pulse.

This one must be a hundred years old
it wears a heavy necklace of stalky green.

That one looks like Ted Hughes
impossibly lofty, swarthy,
with thick arms.

Later, lying in bed alone
you hear the rasping screech of the owl

the scream of something
that flies all night, exhilarated
by the dark, yet terrified
of its own appetite.

The Eye in the Tree

An eye in the bark of the birch – a black, slant iris
etched in a silver spine. A horizontal tear
with a dark corolla, a cracked lancet; spear-shaped
as a fallen bay leaf, bark splitting to spokes
like eyelashes or rays of divine light.

The man staring into the coppice from the rain
shudders. *It's a trick of the eye,* he tells himself.
Thinks of a stain on a wall that looked like a cow,
a cloud that looked like Elvis.

At night in the siding the train stands frozen as a mouse
under a cat's paw. The eye doesn't blink.

There are more eyes in the trees by the motorway
eyes that are etched in deep, as if pitted with sorrow,
hollowed with despair.

The trees breathe in fumes
as the cars scuttle past – a carnival of sick cockroaches
with gaudy shells.

Each tree has one dark eyelet,
deep as a button cut, raw as a fabric gash.

Grey smoke rises to swathe the larynx of the blackbirds.
The trees shake their boughs like widows' hands.

A Murmuration is Seen Above the City

Black spots, iron filings, broken particles,

dark smudges, inked finger prints
pin-prick flurries, smoke plumes

a black scarf painted in pointillist style
a pixelated kaleidoscope
a wave made of dust motes, arching.

Not starlings but politicians –
this fluid mass with one mind.

Cabinet Ministers
morphing and merging,
writhing in the air

wishing that in life
they had acted differently
but airborne, and dead, it is too late.

We look up from Food Banks
to watch the sky teem.

The sky is bruised with the bloated bodies of
Cabinet Ministers

fat from stolen fruit, they eclipse the sun.

We shiver, as we watch them wheel and turn,
our bones almost through our skin.

Happy Hour with Heartache

It's always like this at first, *Heartache*
you prowling in,
modelling your pelage like *haute couture*
scuffing the stools with your talons
as you leap.

Cimmerian creature, Stygian stray – you belong
in this cellar bar, your faltering song
a pathetic torch
in the subterranean dark.

Aren't you beguiling at first?
Lashing yourself to the legs of the other drinkers
with a sleek tail
mewing *My name is Chagrin*, (if anyone asks).

Before long you are picking up crisps
with the hooked papillae of your rough tongue,
lapping beer from the floor,
caterwauling as if on heat.

When your growl weakens to a chitter
I take you home
close the door and lick your fur smooth

slip small segments of raw meat
into your mouth

tuck you up in my bed,
then curl up in the tiny space you have left.

How to Paint a Brexit Angel

They appeared melancholic enough according to Victorian art,
a mystic sadness in their eyes,

holding their symbols out to us in taper-thin fingers
(globes containing the first sinners,
their nakedness - a blunt fact).

They seemed, even then, sickened
by those who had exiled themselves from Eden.

But how to paint them now? With furrowed brow,
the stricken look in the eyes
of a mother visiting a child
who has committed a terrible crime,

and doesn't recognise who he is
doesn't know him any more
though she once wore him under her skin.

The Prophet is Mistaken for a Fare dodging Hipster on the London Overground

Slacker or striver
no one in London wants to wait more than three minutes
for a train
and the station staff are too weary
to give chase to the man with the *Lumber Sexual* look
who leaps over the turnstile, great coat winging out
as if to aid his flight.

Obvs a hipster, everyone thinks
and only the girl who sits opposite him
wonders about the incongruity of his baby soft skin
and the white hairs which run through his black beard
like furrows of snow in cracked earth.

As they reach the city he leans forward
and in an accent she doesn't know
he tells her he has dreamt about

glassy tongues licking houses into blue, children's mouths
gaping like guppies
cracks running through red soil, oceans shrivelled up, babies,
and fish, twitching on arid land.

Where is the parliament
of men and women braying
as others speak of fire and flooding?
He must tell them what he has seen.

He's thrown off the train at Orange Hill. Hasn't a penny
to pay the fare and refuses charity.

He sleeps in a shop doorway, his coat as rough
as a prison blanket.

The Angel of Revelation visits the New Age Centre

The wind chimes aren't the only issue for the *Angel of Revelation*
who, monstrous-sized, has to shoe-horn himself
through the small door, the little metal moons catching in his hair,
the cold and kitsch making him recoil.

Dressed only in a cloud, he can bear the temperature
of the central heating turned up high,
but the scented candles are noxious
with their chemical rendering of *Heaven*.

What whimsy is this, he thinks at the sight of soapstone
cherub angels
wearing their tiny wings like ears grafted to their backs

and the pictures of soft focus blondes,
sprouting feathers from their see-through shirts.

These are not the messengers, he thinks
with these blind eyes, and doll-like limbs.
Their mouths sealed to a pout.

Security comes running when he roars,
his colossal legs planted firmly into the taupe rug
the grey smoke rising from his feet setting off the fire alarm.

It takes five of them to pull him away from the open window
but not in time to stop him yelling at the pigeons, something about

feasting on kings and peasants
eating off the flesh of all men, both free and bond.

Ghosting for Beginners

Having only the suggestion of fingers, ghosts
are unable to embrace the internet.

The impotent *deceased* instead resort
to rustling papers, slamming doors
photo bombing family portraits,
haloing the living with a nebulous haze.

You, however have all the tools to hand.

There's no need to hang around graveyards
with malevolent intent
or hex the air with an ominous waft.

Simply disappear from her twitter feed,
become invisible on her wall,
leave vast gaps between texts.

Imagine how the ghouls will envy you
when you become a spectre on social media.

You can imagine why they are irked,
absence is *their* Calling Card.

Oh gauzy digits
hovering over the keys,
unable to make impression.

Oh ethereal fingers
unable to click in *'un-friend'*.

I said Thomas, There is a Piece of Work About the Ghost

and you are blood-bled as a ghoul.

Thomas, I said, pray put on your dark coat.

Thomas, I said, you are lambent as the harvest moon.
Your linen trousers are ashen, your waistcoat milky-pale.

Pray wear your dark coat.

Thomas, I said
bedevilled men walk the streets,
and their fingers curl around steel.

Thomas, I told him, take heed.
There are those who believe you haunt them.

Thomas, I told him, I do not ask you to dissemble

but there are those who sense a noose
around their necks
but feel no fingers there,

men who imagine the heft
that squats upon their chest to be unearthly.

Thomas I said,
beware their hair trigger hearts.

A man was tried for killing a labourer by the name of Thomas that he mistook for the Hammersmith ghost. The victim's widow had previously warned him that in his white overalls he may be mistaken for a ghoul.

The Ghost Marriage

*As part of the Chinese tradition of Ghost marriage – at the death of her
fiancé, a bride could still go through with the wedding, and the dead
groom could be represented by a white cockerel.*

Finding himself in the afterlife without a wife,
he thinks of his earth-bound love.
How cursed he was to die
only days before his marriage!

Returning to his mother's house
he urges her to arrange a wedding feast,
to bring his *intended* to the table.

A white rooster plays spouse.

The bereaved sits through the ceremony.
She watches as he struts in circles
arrogantly, scratches
at the floor for scraps.

As she dabs at her eyes to blot the tears
her family tell her how fine and upright
his scarlet comb stands,

how she must not recoil
from his rubbery wattle, flinch at the sound
of his scratching spurs.

Later, she will lie in the satin sheets
of her family's dowry as he perches
on the bed head,

clucking and crowing to stake his claim.

The Protocol of Haunting According to Randall and Hopkirk (Deceased)

Dressed quite informally in life, after he's been murdered
he sports a linen suit; cream-coloured and impervious to stains –
even when he's sitting in the turned soil of his own,
recently dug grave.

His partner in tracking-down-crime gets an echoey phone call
asking him to come by the church.
Hopkirk, killed in a hit and run,
miraculously still able to spin the dial of an old Bakelite phone,
wants to meet. Thus begins
the protracted partnership of man and ghoul.

Hopkirk spends his days helping Randall solve cases,
oscillating between teleporting,

and hanging around in the back of the office
where he can see his wife, scarlet carapaces
of her manicured nails tapping at the keys.

Luckily she has no idea that her deceased spouse,
unable to talk to her, still speaks to Randall,
and can even communicate with minor characters.

Randall doesn't flaunt the haunting,
or talk to air in her presence.

She swathes her grief in Dior, dresses routinely in swanky
couture, her platinum hair beaten
with a brush to a glistening plane.

She alone sees herself first thing, hair like a rain cloud,
dank against her tear stained face,

after a night huddling in the hollow
that his absent body has left in the bed.

The Ventriloquist Dolls of the Dead

There's one – slack- limbed
as if its strings had been cut.

Another – opposite you on the train, wooden-faced
with ennui,

suddenly jumping into life, flashing you *that* smile.

Then there's the man on stage with the mouth
which could be on hinges
who jerks abruptly

raises his hand to cover his eyes as he laughs
just like your dad did.

The gestures are identical,
and he's moving as if
he were a dummy

brought out of the box long enough
for your dead dad
to show that even though you can't see his lips move,
he still fancies a chat.

Ghost Horses

Do not think that after death
the Mind dismounts.

Do not think that once the race is run
the Mind puts down the reins.

Do not think that when
our legs have stopped breaking up the turf

the Mind
leads us gently back into the stable
lets us stand in flaxen stalks of grain

or fetlock deep in long grass,
stock-still, our backs a landing stage for birds.

No, after death
the mind will still drive us
ghost horses that we are

our trace hooves skittering
over our old stomping grounds

forced back to the familiar circuits
as *Memory* brings down the whip.

The Ghost room

When the Ghost Room contains you, it is like being flooded
with water
or encased in air.

There are windows in the Ghost Room, and doors,
but your hands cannot make purchase.

The edges of the ghost room are flimsy as tracing paper
but unyielding as brick.

The walls of the Ghost Room are diaphanous but sturdy.

You will still be able to see
the autumn colours blaze,
a friend pass by in a scarlet coat

but you will view it as if through glass.

The Ghost Room is airy and immaterial as this stanza
but it will occupy your thoughts.

Watch a mime artist at work, pushing against the invisible.
He is testing the perimeters of his Ghost Room.

The Ghost Room is the spectre of your childhood realms,
the room in which you read to your dying father.

The Ghost Room was built in the liminal,
your mind drifts toward it at dusk.

The book in the Ghost Room is ethereal.
Its pages are phantom children
joined at the spine.

William Blake Draws the Ghost of a Flea

Blake says the flea complains of a haunting.
He says he will draw the ghost within the flea.

From the darkness of the mahogany board,
Blake exhumes a body.

Not a pinprick creature that could be crushed under the thumb,
but a figure pulvinated with muscle,

a self-vaunting bruiser
standing between two curtains, as if on stage.

It is stocky as an ox, pugnacious,
posed menacingly under an artificial sky.

The flea's ghost has insect eyes, piercing and hard,
a reptilian tongue
encased in a herculean form.

The ghost in the flea laps at a small bowl awash with red.

The ghost of man cannot inhabit a horse
Blake tells the critics.

Imagine the troughs of blood needed
to slake our avid thirst.

*After Williams Blake's painting The Ghost of a Flea – which depicts a
monstrous man, the spirit of whom is trapped within an insect.*

On How Ghosts Take the Moral High Ground

A week after hanging himself he's back,
returned to the house of his fickle lover

shroud-bound, glassy faced, righteous, hovering above her bed
like a see-through falcon, ready to drop on prey.

The noose that did for him is lank as a snake's shed skin,
his tracing-paper fingers claw the air,

and he moans each time she kisses her new paramour
until they split apart, startled.

In life he was licentious,
but after death he's immaculate as a saint

scrubbed clean as if the Spiritual Realm
were a rough sponge brandished by a fierce hand.

All his sins are exfoliated now, his new skin
light as bible paper, lucent as rain.

Pity the poor woman beneath him
too guilt-struck to enjoy another's embrace.

Imagine if each time you kissed a new lover
you were haunted by the one you betrayed.

Imagine if your sin was sent back – fingered,
pale hands holding a candle,

flame a halo around the shaft
so your darkness was broken by their pure white light.

Burying Pan

The hoof juts out, so the vicar digs deep.

The arm goes under – the statue's stone-frozen limb,
flung out to signify ownership of the Arcadia
(once taking in the sweeping lawns,
the faux – forest, the cold plunge pools
in which the Master would wash the stench
of the wenches off) – now points below.

Pan's pipes are soon stopped with dirt.
No more will he call the goddess down
from the sky or hypnotise the herds.

The vicar will work all night if he has to,
scoop soil, flick it over stone.
level the ground with the edge of his spade.

Years later he will forget
what he has buried down there,
and, tempted by a glimpse of the naked moon,

will rush out into the grounds

miss the tip of stone that catches his foot,
and stumble back down into the dark.

*A vicar in Painswick, worried about the effect the goat god would have
on his parishioners, buried a statue of Pan in the grounds of his
Church.*

A Wild Swan in the Tunnel

They had met in her office, and after coffee,
she read him Yeats as rain patters on glass.

The swan brings the sky down with its wings
captures Leda in the rush of air,
in a cage of feather bane and arched neck.

Now he drives her through the tunnel
something swirling
on the car cd, the air conditioning soft as feathers.

A headline has stained his thumb like finger print ink
Killer with a penchant for pale blondes evades capture.

She tells him about a swan found wandering
in the tunnel, how it hissed and reared
when they tried to take it out into the light.

Did the bird imagine the tunnel was a wintered river,
running under rock? Did drivers see a raised wing,
anger in the bird's dark eyes?

The swan's wings are pale as platinum,
glossy as vigorously brushed hair.

Later he lies on his bed and thinks of Leda.

The blow that brought the girl down to earth,
the wings that kept on beating.

How silken the feathers must have felt against her face.

Watching

In the park the cygnets drowse on the edge of the path.

We steer a route to avoid them,
treading lightly, so to not disturb their sleep.

From the twisted boughs of a tree
a rattle we mistake for woodpecker.

A bird's frenetic recitation,
plump swell of belly peppered with speckles, tiny beak
clapping to emit the clatter of sound.

The sky is louring over the lake but where we walk it's still azure
and against the blue the bird is a bright fruit on the bough.

A *storm cock* you say as we stand close enough
to see the feathers flare out like the spokes
of the sun.

How long are we there before we realise
that we have inspired the machine gun call,
that our proximity has stirred the thrush to alarm?

We walk away from the tree on tiptoe.
Our feet barely making an impression on the ground.

Yet I can't resist going back for one more glimpse
of that downy jewel,
telling myself all the time to forget the cost.

Her Mane is Smoke Rising from Rough Land

her teeth an ancient wall. Her nose looks more like a snout
than we expected.

She's nothing like the horses we've seen in our picture books
or the shoe boxes we'd splashed with paint
to resemble dappled flanks.
We watch her jaundiced teeth as she eats.

Her eyes are glossy, darted with a slit, her rough tongue
glossy, engorged – a flailing rope of red.

She's tearing at the grass
as if it were a dress she wanted to remove
and I lean down and harvest for her.

Grafted tightly to the ground the thick stalks
take some plucking,
and I do not see her lower her head
like a boom bar.

The marks she leaves in my back are oval as a friendship circle,
scorching as a ring of fire.

Beyond the Sea

This tinder air could catch like paper. We crave
the breeze that scuttles in across the shore.

We are miles from the coast,
from our little brother, his red bucket
of sand,
the tide kicking up its heels as it dances in.

The gallery is a cool cloister.
In the first room Poussin's paintings rise out
of the dark. We gaze at a blue
as vivid and alluring as a mirage.

The blue born of the Lapis Lazuli
which powdered Cleopatra's eyes,
the amulet celebrated in the book of the dead,

the colour that, according to Kandinsky
calls man to the infinite.

The dazzling ultramarine
that the artist has used for Mary's robes
as she marries Joseph, under the eyes of God.

There is the sea! We point at the painting.
There it is – pooling, in the Virgin's skirts.

The name for ultramarine blue comes from the Latin ultramarinus
which literally means beyond the sea.

A Complaint about the Traffic

And then the skylark breaking out of the earth,
barrel body plump as the rain-ripe clouds,

climbing steeply, song rising to a tower
one long, liquid warble, and strident *preet*.

Just the two of us on the crest of the hill, halted
in our heavy steps,
our clamorous complaints about the traffic
and this bird, its quick startled cry transfixing us
as it hovers above like an angry ghost claiming tenure.

We are dying out, it could be saying or simply
step away from the nest!

That skylark's alarm call, as it rose, as if scooped up to the sky!

It could be telling us about the fledgling Blackbird
we will encounter on the side of the road

half down, half feather,
eyes shut as if dreaming of flight
tiny legs like broken twigs
beak matted red from where it hit the car.

The Hedgehog

Do we love it more for looking like us,
but prettier, with its dark, inquisitive eyes,
the delicate fingers with their long slender nails?

It's lying on the verge, flies glinting
on its back like emerald brooches.

At first we think it is sleeping
eyes sealed, paws clasped together,
an aunt holding her favourite bag.

But the legs don't look right.
They are crushed into its belly
as if it has run into a wall.

There's no blood to suggest road kill
and there's other ways it could have died.

On the way back we peer at it again.
It looks like an old woman
curled up in bed, or recoiling from a kick.

You suggest starvation – or that pollution
has killed the insects it would eat.

You move it gently on to its front
so it turns back into a globe,
a spiked planet – bristling.

Sowing Seeds

The papers in the hotel are full of the President
who thinks climate change is a hoax.
Headlines say *It's Game Over for Planet Earth.*

You take me to your fields where feral goats chew cud
and you tell me how you are planting yellow rattle
to suppress the rough grasses growth.

The ground is still tussocked but you talk
about meadow flowers, wild legumes,
the bovine hooves that cut open the swathe.

I tell you about the President and you say
when the waters rise London will become Atlantis.

A white horse, stately as Pegasus, watches us
as we stumble down the slope to the shore.

We are still talking about the earth's future
as we leave footprints on the sand.

The sea, its salty tongue working
like someone who will not stop speaking,
gets the final word.

Befriending the Butcher

When my father first walked in to the shop,
the pheasant dangling clumsy from a string like a plummy yo-yo,
and asked the butcher to prepare it for the pot,
he didn't expect to hear Mozart playing. Or to talk Kierkegaard

as the feathers were plucked. A Thomas Hardy hero
striding the coast before work,
chin cleft like the rocks at the estuary edge,
we thought he'd mark the whole country with his steps.

He spent his days dressing flesh
and his nights – carving wood,
reading brick-heavy biographies of Larkin or Keats.

Good health didn't last till retirement.
We visited him in a bungalow on the other side
of the tracks, his hand-carved bird tables trembling
on long stalks as the trains thundered past.

There we sat, over-shadowed by Victorian furniture,
none of that blood-bled modern stuff,
just oak, or mahogany,

on chairs as dark and immense as the Wagner
which poured into the room, slowed down

by its own heft. Around us – shelves of Folio editions
fat spines emblazoned gold
row after row of corpulent companions
in brass and buttoned regalia.

No longer able to walk, he scored the floor
with wheel chair marks as if ticking items off a list

and the single bar of the fire was a winter sunset;
a thin scarlet line, blazing with its own heat
as it slipped down silently, into the dark.

A Journey

All the way to Paignton the dog panting, eyes bulging
like stones pushed through putty, tail beating a military tattoo
against my leg, the man at the other end of the lead
inked from head to foot, a spider's web protruding
out from under his collar like iron spokes
the two women who aim to get *annihilated*
when they reach 'Spoons, shrieking,
their shrill words hanging over our heads like drones
the men crushing cans of Polish lager, threatening to lynch
the next bloke they see in the railways insignia,
and I'm not wanting to ask the dog to move its arse off my foot
for fear of upsetting the owner
who says he left the SAS for *Medical Reasons,*
then standing by the loo all the way to the country station
protected at least, from the sight of a fight that starts
in *First.* Finally arriving at the one track station,
the trees bowing down in homage to a sky
which sprinkles rain onto our faces like holy water
and my brother arriving in our father's old car
full of wood, twigs scattered across the seats
moss in the ashtrays, leaves under the brake pedals,
and it's as if he had brought the forest to us and we all exhale.

On reading *Love is a Dog from Hell*

Bukowski's vision is bald as a bulb
with the shade removed.

His language is blunt, his lines as short
as a shopping list.

The man you spent the weekend with
is locked into your head like a forked fox knot.

In the first poem Bukowski lies in bed staring at a fly
that circles a cold takeaway. A strip of pork glistens.

The room's walls are unadorned. The grey day
leers through the slats.

Bukowski thinks of how it's always a long road back to the self,
afterwards.

The staccato of each expression is a brutish axe chop.

Yet occasionally, a longer sentence unfurls
about how tender that first kiss,

as if the heart had briefly written
before the flesh grabbed back the pen.

We Didn't Know

as we lay, green blades
against our throats, crickets ticking
in the long grass like invisible clocks

or when we ignited our kinder tongues
with spirits, leapt up.

We still didn't know,
when we slaked our droughty mouths
heads beneath the rusty tap like horses

or stood swathed in grey plumes
swallowed salty minnows of pink flesh.

We still didn't know, as we shrieked
at a ravaged pirate
clasping a sword to a paint stain on his chest.

We still didn't know, when a sudden squall rushed us like flotsam
to the warmth of our flats

where we switched on our phones
to read the first messages *I am Safe, I am safe.*

But we knew then, when we scanned the news
eyes quick as forest fire

read about the girl who cried
save me save me,
ten times
before the blade went in.

And that night dreaming of the man falling towards us
arm reaching out, red stain on his shirt opening up

until every inch of his soft cotton shirt was a glistening red.

The Visitation

When we first saw it – a translucent pelt,
fast as electricity racing up a cable, a fuzz darting
behind the chest of drawers, we talked of ectoplasm,
of the ghosts of mice

and remembered how, not long after dad died
a tower of books tumbled like a house of cards.

Later we see droppings, a flash of fur. We shriek,
more frightened now we know it's real.

It's the flesh and blood that spooks us.
Not the whisper in the next room,
the airborne gauze, the glassy aura.

It's the heft of things, the boulder and ballast
of life, the weight of grief, that we drag behind us like an iron
limb.

Haunted

Emily's is a Romantic poet, head haloed by conch shell curls
soprano voice berating the boys who bullied him at school,
or bewailing his untimely saline death.

Jennie's ghost is just a sound
a girlish laugh that even her neighbours have heard.

It's what you would expect in an old house, she says,
a ghost goes with the beams.

Anthea's is on all fours, see-through
but giving the impression of black
like rain made pit by the winter night.

She describes a ridged back with wings
thick legs, a pugilistic stance
and scuttling.

What haunts you? My friend asks.

I have no animal
or little girl to speak off, no poet
back from the dead

but there is this-
some nights I swear I hear the whispering
of a disembodied mouth

as if *Time* herself was muttering to me
about all that I have lost.

Fallen

In the orchard,
her tongue turns to cuckoo spit
at the sight of the overripe damsons
lying in the long grass.

They should have been plucked
long ago, he says.

His fingers gleam with honeyed juice
as he feeds her, then worms his tongue
into the pulp within her mouth.

As he steals her sweetness
the fallen fruit, their skins split from impact,
weep a glitter into the ground.

So it Doesn't Fly Away

From where I stand your hair
looks like a nest of gold.

You are kneeling down to talk to an artist
as he works furiously on a picture of a crow.

A child could have done that, I snap
and the artist turns to me – eyes lucid as rock pools.

All day you have tried to hold my hand
but you look like a Renaissance Angel in a beanie hat
and I don't want anyone to think you are my son.

He is telling you about the rook he reared,
the blackbird that *kissed him*
and kissed him better than any girl.

Last night I flinched
when you touched me.

Have you ever had a robin land on your hand?
Its little legs are lighter than twigs.
You have to keep your hand steady.

You are both looking at me, when the artist says that.

You have to be gentle, he says, *so it doesn't fly away.*

At Rame Church

A spire rises through the trees like a finger held aloft
in admonition.

Giddy after taking a corner too fast
we tumble giggling out of the car
crush long blades beneath our feet,
break a path through the overgrown.

No bird song, or conversation.
The graves mouth their names like mutes.

A grate in the church's door
prevents the entry of birds
but larger, and without wings, we enter.

How tight lipped the tombs are, on death.
We run hot fingers over their inscriptions
as if Braille.

Later, as the sun ghosts the cool stone,
I pluck a blackberry from the bramble
which crowns a child's grave.

How bitter it tastes, having been taken too early.

Salvo

These lanes are wounds that never heal.

We open the earth's scar,
our boots hoofed with mud and clay.

December, between Dog and Wolf, the air is furred,
a bristle burn against our skin.

We've walked through forests,
algae light sluicing through the trunks,

past trees stripped back to vein and sinew,
boughs exalted, still singing of the lightning blast.

And now the hail, pellets from a ghost gun,
moon-shot, white as new teeth,
bone-hard and glassy.

Winter's salvo
bombarding our exposed flesh,
until, unarmed, we run for cover.

Yet in the shelter of the sunken wood
white gold on the trees,

dun browns alchemised to precious metal
and the ground covered in the sky's scattered pearls.

My skin still smarts from the hit
of the hail. Like love,
how it dazzles, while it burns.

The Song

The ivy is lustrous with rain
the path beneath us a morass
of mud and leaf. My father's voice warbles
with joy.

You talk too much,
my mother says, wraps
his emerald scarf around his mouth
to stop the cold reaching his heart.

His eyes, bright green as algae
and flooded through with light,
beam above a muffed smile.

Was it then we heard the robin
singing from the heart of a tree?

Soft rain spluttering on leaf,
twilight deepening in the woods,
the bird's song becoming bolder as the night fell.

Returning alone, I can hardly bear to listen
to that bluster, to the urgent song of a creature
asserting its claim on a darkening earth

A Ghost Before Dawn

The future cannot come without the grace of setting things aside
                                                            John Burnside

Here at owl light, is the husband,
brought back by the widow's tight grip
and backward glance.

He's luminous as a jack-o'-lantern, gauzy and glittering
as a spider web in rain.

But this filmy, limpid creature,
is too ethereal to embrace,

disorientated as a traveller
who wakes from a slumber to a strange town.

She would do best to leave him in the liminal,
glimpse him in a dust shimmer,
feel his presence as breath upon the skin.

We could learn from Orpheus
about letting go,

but instead our desires are gravity
holding the dead
fixed down to the earth.

How will morning come when the
night's scent still hangs heavy on the air
unseasonable as honeysuckle in winter?

How can we hear the one note of the dawn
when night is still whispering in our ears?

And Who Will Speak of the Ghost of the Rain

the spirits of the silver birches,
the traces of honeysuckle, the lily's souls?

We paint the spirit world as limbed and familiar,
describe a woman in jellyfish-bell
of crinoline skirt, gliding,

a drowned boy glistening with the lake that finished him,
a little girl, frothy with lace, clutching a doll,
skin glossy and grey as mercury spill.

But what of the spectre of cat,
darting under the door, like a vacuum-sucked flame,

the ghost moth, cocooned in its own gauzy blur,
the dead rose misted with its own mane?
What of the abstract other world?

Who dreams the rain's phantom in an arid land,
or writes of the spirit of the air – the grassy fragrance
plaintive amid the pollution – a bitter-sweet ballad
sung softly, under the breath.